LOGAN
STONE

LOGAN
STONE

D. M. THOMAS

Cape Goliard Press
in association with
Grossman Publishers New York

Some of these poems have appeared in the follow-
ing: New Worlds, London Magazine, The New York
Times, Phoenix, P.E.N. New Poems 1967, Encounter,
Transatlantic Review, Priapus, Outposts, Cornish
Review, The Observer, and Poetry Now (BBC).

This first edition was designed, printed and pub-
lished by Cape Goliard Press, 10a Fairhazel Gardens,
London NW6; of this edition 50 copies have been
signed and numbered by the author.

Printed in Great Britain.

Photographs: Gabri Naseman

UK ISBN: paper 0206-00658-6; cloth 0206-00557-1
US SBN: paper 670-43613-5; cloth 670-43612-7; LCCCN: 70-14

COMPUTER 70:
DREAMS & LOVEPOEMS

she is pleased excited by the handsome powerful and older man
who drives masculine and arrogant   with as firm a skill
and watchful care as though it might be a thousand minuteman
warheads couched in their steel burrows   obedient   to the will
of his left hand   guiding and adjusting   and
the closed air full of the song of suave flesh
wined under smooth party dress his right hand
hovered over complicitly tensioned synchromesh
the windscreen   framed the night a radar screen
where only innocent objects and familiar flashed
roadsign   a dead hedgehog trees   a risen moon
but risen nothing that could perturb he clashed
gears tyres and brakes turned right an arrowing road the springs
rode easily catlights disappeared she feline settled   a ridge
they leapt   drenched in excitement   her scented   underthings
flesh steel upholstery talk one rocket-head   a bridge
reared up she drowned in her surrender to the waiting dunes
she had no answer to nor failsafe to the embrace   beneath
isolating intimating night   she was the undine moon's
penetrable hymen   she sought a star   a breath

1

Your thighs meshed in the glow
of the instrument panel,
a gravitational field
drawing eye and hand;
intransigent flow
of digits, mile on mile;
man in the dead of the moon
tonight; hedgehog dead on the road,
flesh whirled on michelin;
images that time
alone must reconcile.

who is this lady dawnembarking at gravesend so belle and blanche the mast-
lights of a passing merchantman glided behind and through   her gloved
hand given to the poet muffled   & gasping for breath   *she will not last
the voyage* he confided   *he is more ill than I* she whispered moved
against his heart he carried a stone cornelian
heavy and cold as the lightyears he would spend
unpillowed on the breasts   of Fanny Brawne
now the lady belle and blanche   at gravesend
rises to accompany endymion his last autumn moon voyage becalmed
in each breath's painful hopeful channel   he watched his actual
migration glassed in her hatches wide her blood seethed   slammed
in storms he fainted scarcebreathed   its meaning he could not fail
she is the wake his name will slide
into   the chaos of unwritten poems
Fanny   that still unravished bride
came Lulworth & a lull   gleams
by *Maria Crowther's* anchorage   a star
the lady   unsupported can barely stand
consumed by   themselves   all they are
they walk the dark sand   stone in hand

Dying, she is not also
well
today: an extra pallor.
Delicately
from tree of ovaries, tree of lungs,
bloodleaves fall
into soft linen.
So like my mother.
I pun savagely
for her. She presses upon me
painfully. The ship that bears
me is *Maria Crowther*,
woman.

If I had not
grown cold
at the last, (you said),
the figures on the urn had lost
all that they hold, withhold.

Swallows gather but they will return.
Already your face is hard for me to compose.
Your lock of hair; your white cornelian stone.

From the first kiss, all is clear:
Severn will sketch the death's head, to keep awake.
And I shall hold
the stone,
cornelian.

Already with thee
the night is tender.
Who?

Could I but dream
this girl was you,
I should get well,
I should return.

3

Tonight I love you as the dashboard gleams
the perfect running of a million parts.
We are two people sharing the same dream,
an upholstered journey sleepier than seconal,
and to no end beyond its own fulfilling.
As soft upholstery loves the bodywork
it couches in; as the steel clip and
narrow black garter-band
loves
the refined and runnable threads they are pulling
with a tolerant intolerance of stresses, as
the mirror loves
the silence into which our future flashes.
The dream is where our love concludes and starts.
My love tomorrow I may stumble saying your name.

she watched it dully from her bed   the phone never stopped ringing
shambling polarbears   or Amundsen and Peary by a flag that streamed
a cyclonic absence of wind   the phone never stopped ringing
one huge step for man thankyou brief a presidential smile gleamed
thank you   thank you   yes a wonderful day for us all
they were halfway through EVA   extra-vehicular activity
once she whispered   agitatedly   no that's impossible
mustn't come   please   no I don't know when it can be
impossible to be private even for a moment
they were   setting up   the seismometer
her eyes   were watching   the shadowy event
while her hand reached   for the vibrator
from the crater sides they picked up lumps of rock
it climbed her breasts   and stiffened   nipples
Houston reported it had received preliminary shock
waves   her body recorded a shrug of   ripples
there was no time for madness to touchdown each second of the count
was counted   the phone interrupted her   thank you thank you
the vibrator infiltrated taut pyjama briefs   over the venerean mount
exploring finding nothing   into a cave   her eyes withdrew

4

I walked upon that lunar sea,
a second Adam to the flood;
the desert called Tranquillity
battered with meteorites. I stood,

as in Korea or Vietnam.
A barren plain that's drunk its gore.
In heaven too, I saw, the Ram
is slaughtered in a slower war.

Seconal was my only peace,
patented on our own dark star;
oxygen was love; to find out this,
strange, that I had to fly so far.

Unfiltered the sun's furnace roared;
a shadow was its fierce extreme;
a saviour round my body poured
cool water of Siloah's stream.

Even as the fish who rose to us
bore its own sea into our veins,
if we embrace the universe,
we must bring trees, we must bring rains.

We must bring dreams. I walked on ground
not sanctified by joy or sin.
Dream-emptiness stretched all around.
I wondered when life would begin.

Each second crammed with robot task;
EVA, the shadow I pursued;
tried to shut out, behind my mask,
the solitude's deeper solitude.

My rib in pain, as though some Eve
would spring, I slept but fitfully.
I felt it sad that I must leave
only my footprints on the sea.

5

To turn left, to turn right;
through me not myself alone
but a whole continent moves,
a world; the Old Glory planted on that moon
tonight; under the ice-cap polaris roves.
Every decision has to be right,
and without hesitation or remorse;
with this movement of a hand I set in motion
an irretrievable course;
even if it is wrong it will be right.
Even if I turn left, it will be right.
Fear adds salt, the velvet engine hums
adrenalin elation. Right.

6

A full moon rising over Finland
set the radar screens flickering holocaust.
Your crossed legs' nylon threads'
rising moonlit field of forces
unleashes a warhead.

7

I open the locket,
touch the lock of plain brown hair,
lock
so soft and so unopenable.
Fire fiercer than the consumption that
burns me burns me

when from his eyes' portent-hungry observatory dome
despairing calculations reckoned that his universe
was running out was racing for all its gathering momentum
of spirit its perpetually thickening noosphere round desire's
core to meet head-on that anti-universe counter-time and -charge blight
to the wheat he should have strolled nonchalantly down from the snow-
line picked fruit in the fields then they might
have survived the impact indeed her troubled face begged him to do so
instead he panicked the blood's launching-pads submitted her
to the pressure of thrice-ten gravities strapped in
through space-warp headed for the metagalactic centre
mercilessly the cunt-vortex his desperation burning adrenalin
dervish dance of galaxies catherine wheels of stars the womb
hoping like Diarmuid and Grania Lancelot and Guinevere
whom they saw there white stunned in their goldprowed tomb
and Tristan and his Iseult in the black ship that there
where it began its end might be delayed by a few micro-
seconds but no he had dug his own grave hearts
thumped at the last the Word going out she strapped below
him reaching hopelessly into her new dimension new start

8

Your hair
black, black as the dead, wrong side of the moon,
comet tresses,
if my lips dare probe them, electrically alive as a storm of meteors,
and as mortal to my peace of mind,

elipsed by darkness, the whites of your eyes gleam at me
like the coronae of a binary eclipse,
the cold, still chastity of your thighs where my teeth wander
is the Milky Way, galactic whirlpool and forge
which comes to us as cold, still, chaste light;

the constellations crazy,
their patterns haywire;
in the space of a week
you have flared from nothing into a supernova.

9

She touches her vagina;
and turns her gaze to the moon's blankness

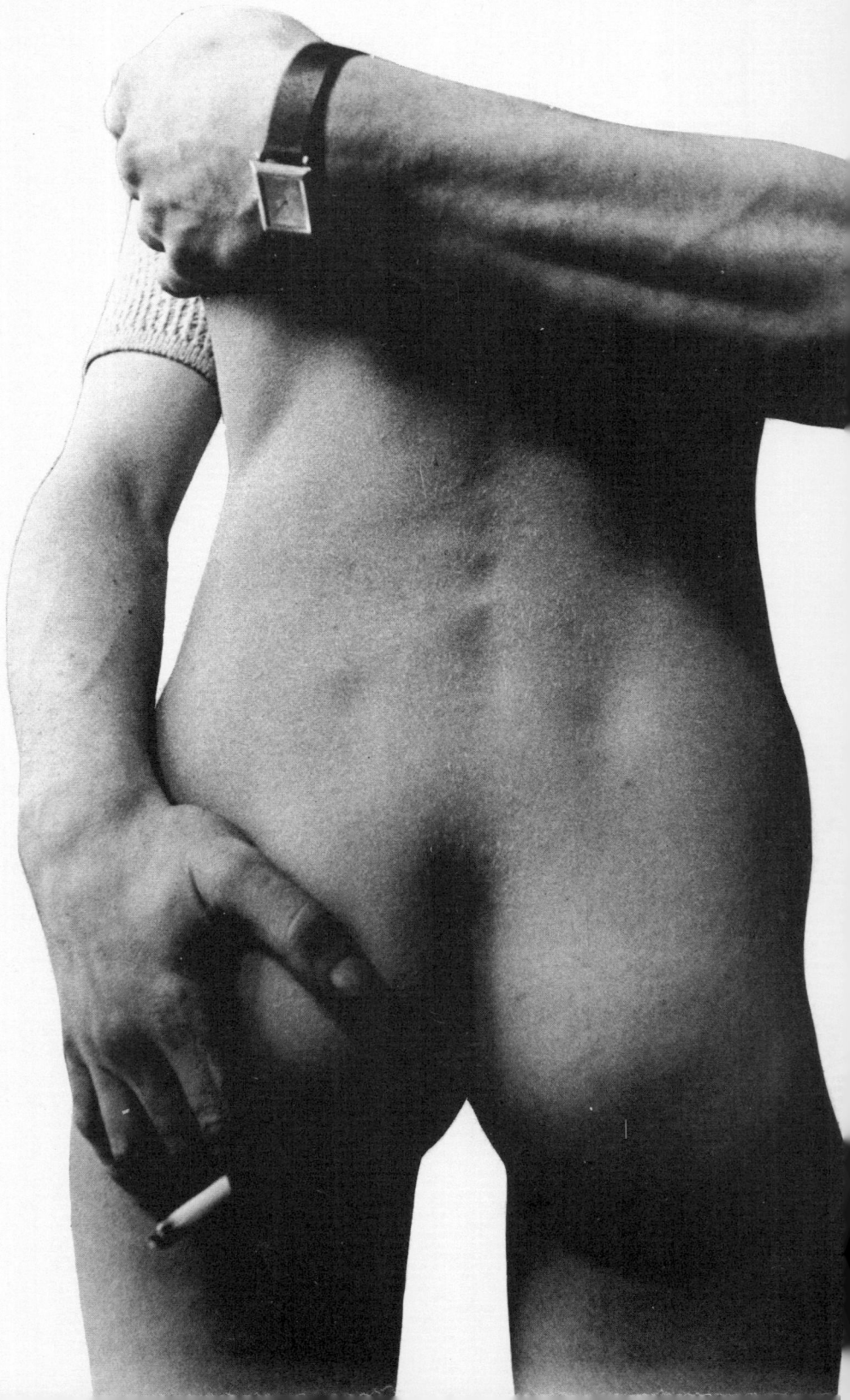

Ophelia in your party-dress
the automobile's
skirts of steel,
heavy with their drink,
have pulled you to an unmelodious
and evil lay.

You are a flower crushed
on a dynastic battlefield;
you interrupted the swordthrust
meant for a greater.
Your death was doubtful;
you have become a brawl

over your maimed rites; an expendable sting
in an old curse, an argument
over your virgin crants;
but from your fair
polluted flesh
violets will spring.

Since you, my matchless donor, cut
me off as you cut off your hair,
—romantic folios you must shut,
hunting for more prosaic styles,—
hacking it, dropping it in the fire,
the ripening bounty of three years
caught in the same tongue as my letters:
I take your letters and I cut
lying phrases from each page,
re-make them, strip on burning strip,
into each day a new collage,
a letter passionate and long,
re-seal it in an envelope
invisibly along the edge,
the flap still sealed from your moist tongue,
and send your letters to myself.

Since you, my soul and transplant, cut
me off like a long distance call
that ate into your youthful purse,
chequebook of marriageable beauty,
before I could pretend to reverse
the charge of love to my account,
mid-sentence in a blackmail plea,
as on the night I drove, through tears
contained by the mesmeric screen's
sickled, blindly springing rain,
your wraith still with me in the car
that you would never ride again;
coins became tranquillizers, call-
boxes dressing-stations, scarlet
along the highway, and to hear
your rising anger, easier than
the enormity of your withdrawal;
I made it grow, from each dead town;
all response gone, my ear still caught
some comfort in the throbbing phone,
I knew its green shape in your hall;
then, off the hook, at least it was
your air's indifference that spoke;
in a dark time I grasped at straws:

since all your lines went dead to me,
the hour each week your call came through
I arrange to get a call from time;
he rings reminding me it is
the hour I can expect your voice;
time who interrupted you
from me, and dragged all cables down,
makes small amends; you ring and ring;
time's tone was never pure like this;
for a wild minute love is true.

nine G.I.'s swinging down the rough road to Xuan Ngoc
where a full moon is shining floods the paddy fields
around it Surveyor turns like the point of a clock-
hand   spin-off from that arrogance falls
onto the nine G.I.'s nearing the hamlet of Xuan Ngoc
they rough up eight huts and in the ninth prepare
a girl for ritual rape but under flashlight they look
closely long at her cunt and diagnose VD they spare
her and go to the tenth hut they find the young mother no harm
in her and place on father sister and two children a guard
outside her skinny resigned flesh has been nurtured on napalm
five have already screwed her and the next two inside are hard
when the father sets up a screeching howl and they grow afraid shoot
all five next morning it is a chance of war the major forgives
spin-off from a skirmish with VC the five-year girl stirs butt
of an M-14 smashes the story perfect except the mother lives
five G.I.'s swing down the dirt-track to Cat Tuong
where a full moon is shining on the paddy fields
collect in the hamlet a peasant-girl to take along
to share their five-day mission and their meals

Be great to fuck you on the dunes
where nothing grows but dry sandgrass,
your face a wayside stone of runes.

Lit by the headlights and the moon's
our instants throng on us and pass.
Be great to fuck you on the dunes.

Hand groping thigh, the future swoons
like a nude patient under gas;
your face a wayside stone of runes.

Midnight and engine-warmth maroons
us on Steel Island ringed by glass.
Be great to fuck you on the dunes.

Viola-husked the engine croons
monotones enigmatic as
your face. A wayside stone of runes

flicks by; the sharp rear-mirror prunes
from glare of might-be drifts of was.
Be great to fuck you on the dunes,
your face a wayside stone of runes.

13

i

This final privacy:
in love or war
to be shot
surrounded by cameramen.

Wait! Freeze.
A camera-plate is broken.
A fly settles on sweat.

ii

Colour-supplement
for a grey sunday;
Hollywood-jungle-technicolour.
Concentratedly,
staring down, this vietnamese
girl, man-handled, does up her
shirt-button;
her bewildered, lively, almost-
dead child on her arm.
It is
obscene of her.
No one should be shot
fastening a shirt-button
ten seconds before being shot,
(triangle of firm brown flesh).

whisper now   je t'aime   slide your hand to meet his   so
lean over him   draw your hair back from where it veils your mouth
kiss him   where passion is edged with nuances of boredom   throw
your thigh across his   in amends   lustfully   talk about truth
in alphaville   your voice as close
to his ear as this hidden receiver
is to yours   the lens will trace
intimately   the fall of the tear
that you will now evoke   I will zoom right in
truth in alphaville make up your own dialogue
whisper   while I whisper do you recall the inn
high in the mountain   and higher still   the log-
cabin where we sheltered   my ring then on your finger
till you lost it in the snow and we scrabbled on our knees   fill
your round tear with that slope and those cedars   I will linger
on it   while you talk   to your lover   of truth in alphaville
then   we will cut   to an empty afternoon   cinema   rendezvous
with him   distrait   unkempt and late   you will watch this scene
then   cut to the premiere of this   where with your new
husband we shoot you watching you & your lover watching you on the screen

I watch you, glacial in mink,
enter on the arm of your husband,
imperious through the sighs
of your fans, the autographs.
Haughty, you take your seat;
your arm shrinks from his hand;
I whisper into your ear,
I am still crazy for you.
   Mink is as tender as steel
   in alphaville.

He is still crazy for you.
He watches you, late, uncombed,
with lateness on your mind
straight from your doctor's room,
enter the cinema's dark
afternoon, sit straight by him.
Neither yet flickers a sign.
You brush your hair from your eyes.
   Hair is as molten as steel
   in alphaville.

He watches you watching the screen
With never a glance at him.
He watches him loving you,
je t'aime je t'aime je t'aime
he whispers, now as then.
He is still crazy for you.
Your hands touch on the sheet,
like pack-ice, split again.
   Days are as cool as steel
   in alphaville.

Love is a cutting-room, all
images equally true,
I mix them all up in you,
au revoir becomes *je t'aime*
in the crystal at your ear,
as I direct your hand
to stretch for husband, lover;
the camera is crazy for you.
   A film can be cut like steel
   in alphaville.

Your hands in the pit of your back,
steel grapples to eyes of steel;
your breasts on hoardings star;
swiftly you brush your hair;
your husband is crazy for you.
Our son must be fetched from school.
Blinds of the late afternoon
are falling one by one.
    Light opens on the steel
    evening of alphaville.

You are the bathroom-scale's
bland mutability;
the steel tape whips around
your breasts, your waist, your thighs,
imexorably as lovers;
the tape is crazy for you,
erecting your rasped nipples;
it hugs you into despair.
    You ghost into the steel
    slimlines of alphaville.

When, next autumn, next spring,
the houselights go down on this film,
who will be crazy for you,
whispering *je t'aime je t'aime?*
I whisper this in your ear:
stretch out your hand to him,
but remember our mountain-cabin;
preserve it in snow of your tear;
    converse on what is real
    in alphaville.

You are light falling on breasts,
you are a stocking's stretch,
you are the heel of a shoe,
you are a brush through hair,
you are a collar turned up,
you are the leaves you crunch,
you are the wheel of a car,
life is in love with you;
    you are the sad, steel thrill
    that steals through alphaville.

the tinted lenses   swimming on Clara's tears
cleared some of the sting from lying too long
closed   loved   myopia   from Helen's years
in the micro-library bequeathed this her along
with the mark each side her nose the itch behind
her ears the flesh on hips from her alter's food
habits   eight days could not completely   unwind
the thread another person wound she lay in nude
abandonment to her grief   this can't go on
he already suspects I don't take my drugs   I spoke your name
in my sleep   the clock accused   two hours ago she should have gone
to a shifting-booth   mention of his alter reddened with shame
his cheeks two hours ago *he* had shifted out on time
as ever   he sighed with guilt but spoke consolingly
our love   in olden days   would have been no crime
married lovers   with no split   personality
he gazed long in her eyes   they were blinking in pain
danger signals flashed madly   they were Helen's eyes
lens-maddened   his wife had broken shift to catch   to gain
time he shifted too   a stiff alien between moist alien   thighs

15

Ten o'clock and I have tossed
a last beer back out of the ice-box,
turned off the colour picture
and entered the bedroom with her,
a colour picture in her blue nightgown.
The spunk is the same,
when I remember the woman in Xuan Ngoc,
if that was its name.

Da mi basia mille, deinde centum,
take, cut; take, cut: always something
dein mille altera, dein secunda centum,
ever-so-slightly imperfect sets us trying again;
deinde usque altera mille, deinde centum,
sustained by the silence of many held breaths;
vivamus, mea Lesbia, atque amemus,
and if at times another voice whispers
soles occidere et redire possunt,
in your ear or mine, we are professionals,
nobis cum semel occidit brevis lux,
stretch out our hands again and again, to touch;
nox est perpetua una dormienda.
I think we shall perfect it in the grave.

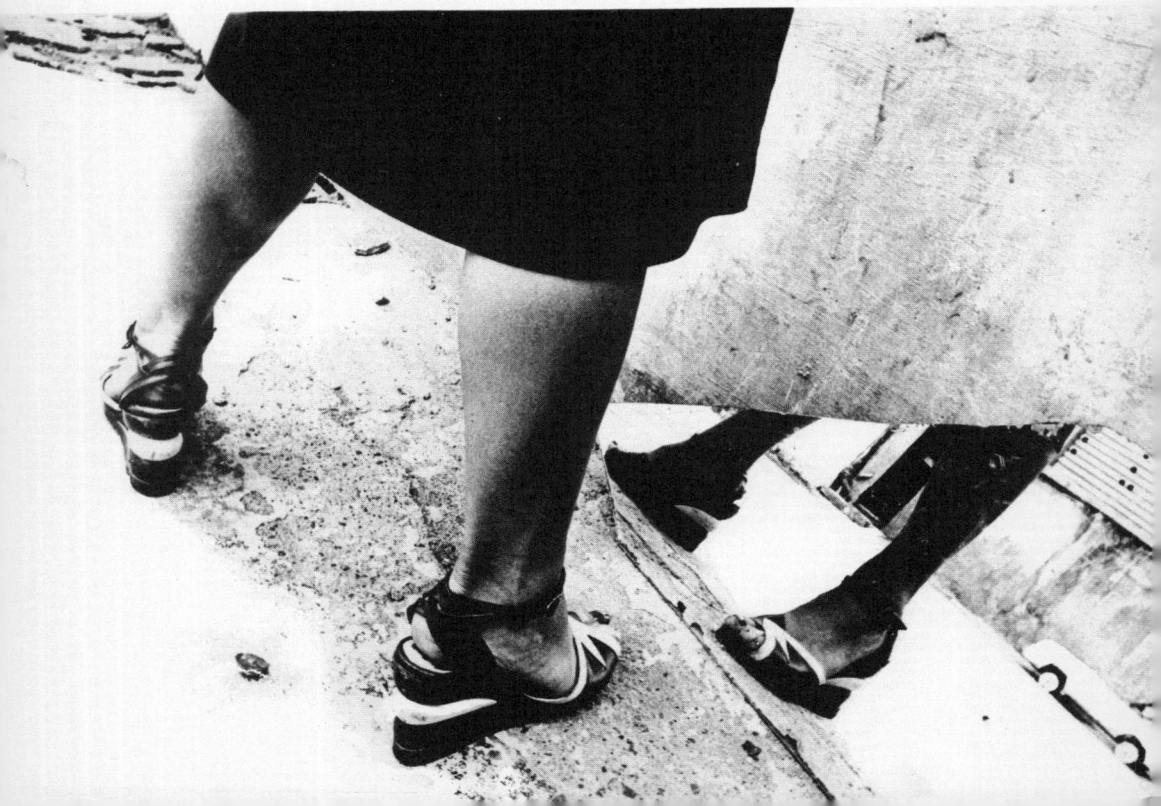

17

As though inside a shifting-booth
where people come to change their truth,
(in every megalopolis,
at every corner of every street
but most where market-alleys meet
plate-glassed boutiqued emporia, this
structure accosts your eyes, and lures),
you sit before ambiguous mirrors,
and take your glasses off, and rub
your eyes, and place to cornea
the plastic lens, and feel freer
already for the change; you stub
your cigarette out, and roll some pot,
playing it cool who once played hot;
fading indents in each brown welt,
you peel your stockings and unhook
—cinchmarks around your waist, your back
stippled—the red suspenderbelt,
roll on your tights, feeling freer
already for the change; no leer
on tube or pillion penetrates
you now, your cunt becomes a crutch
all eyes may see but not too much
intrude on: nothing devastates
the voyeur like a total show,
gone the erotic veils; you grow
a new and space-edge decade; wrap
a mini round you; squat, remove the cap,
and take a pill that won't confine;
you zip on knee-high boots; you wash
bright lipstick off, and draw a fresh
but coolly naturalistic line;
your hair accepts a wig, a mass
of ringlets; cool as menthol grass
you step out of the shifting-booth,
where people come to change their truth,
(in every suburb of every city,
at every corner of every street,
but most where redbrick avenues meet
the overpass, the motorway.)
If I no longer love you, blame
not the shifting counters, but the game;
look younger down the killing years;
blame dust the wind and traffic fling
to lodge under lenses and to sting,
for your lachrymae rerum, tears.

Why does the steel, hygienic city
hold so much dust?
Driving, to fetch my son from school,
tears streaming down my face,
will the curious indifferent standers-by
know it is a contact lens
and not despair?
Agonised, I flick it into my hand
light as a waterdrop. Light.
Water-baby, it swims on the dead sea
of eyes.

Once, on the slopes of Mont Blanc,
I rubbed my eye unconsciously and
it flicked away, joined all the other snow-crystals
in the immense glacier,
till judgement.

Frozen, inseparable,
plastic and tear.
Longer than anyone
it will mourn for me.

we touched the world through the oily palms
of mute petrol salesmen   in forest garages
we saw no headlines sowing   unreal alarms
adjudged danger by our own   steady gauges
what did we care in our favourite layby that the car
radio cut out in the midst of Scarlatti   our lips
neverbreaking our hearts still as near   and   as far
down the short wave band   we followed   the eclipse
but on friday the scarlet lipstick you produced as you prepared to leave me
turned black on your lips   saturday your skirt was no longer orange a blue
moon shone through the windscreen on sunday   on monday we crossed a city
where contrite hymnsinging shook the stadium   whether the lights said   go
we could not tell   till we reached the no-speedlimit sign
tears did not cease to run your eyeshadow not green but ash
on tuesday   the sky was grey   with a black sun
and today at noon there is no colour except   a splash
of violet where your suspenderbelt arches round
a tuft of darker shadow   the shortest wave will
exceed these trees soon   we wait   no sound
lit by black beams   a breeze strums the aerial

19

Your face, beside me in the car and staring ahead,
has the beauty of the austere geometry
of gridroads, highways, underpasses, I
have cut from, imposed on, your innocent terrain.

Though tears star your cheeks like the few
rainsplashes left by the wiper on the windscreen,
the tears of foetuses, perhaps,
we cannot stop—the shoulder is hard.

Must lick up the cat's-eyes, endlessly,
as we do acts of love, slake our hungers where we pause.
The space between what I would like to give you, my
darling, and what I can, is this V, dividing a motorway

into two. One day you will slip away,
save yourself, as a car turns down a sliproad and
is gone. Then, I shall press my foot down
on the accelerator, harder, harder, and be gone.

20

I insist on watching you
piss. You laugh at my insistence.
If I knew why, I would know
the secret of the Mozart piano concerto
that has faintly followed us up the stairs.
How gaily, inexorably, it pursues its coda!

21

You sleep,
uncomfortably. The car dreams
it holds bedrooms, dining-rooms, sun-rooms and creches.

22

This model with her shaven head,
her lustreless and lidless eyes,
erects erotic fantasies
more than your softness in my bed.

She's disciplined as a poem; no sigh
like you exhale, no quickened breath;
coldly she sees—that life, that death,
the curious, pausing passers-by.

Two arms undress her, not her own,
out of a backcloth, black-magician;
you move to order, for coition;
her flesh is hard as bone;

intractable, it gives no aid
to hands that strip the coat, the frock,
unclasp the stockings and unhook
bra and suspenderbelt; you made

your strip too clean, as though the act
of love was why we came. You raced
out of your tights, and I embraced
the four bare stenuous limbs of fact.

If I'd this model in my bed,
never would imagination die;
hard-on from rasp of clothing, I
would never take her maidenhead.

23

When we lie together
meltingly
as the swan with Leda,
your eyes grow overfull
with children in Biafra,
children in Vietnam.
I am that brutal soldier,
my tenderness is rape.

All afternoon,
among stereos, plush carpets, among breasts and buttocks,
I have been making love to your eyes,
where it has been snowing frenziedly
and clearing to blue skies.
Your eyes have the stereogram's
mysterious fidelity,
that rises when I draw near,
fades when I move away.
My whisper caught in the one groove
of I love you,
like the old gramophone used to do.
All afternoon I have been making love to your eyes.
Now as we say goodbye,
and plan to meet tomorrow,
the snow has melted, retracted
into brambles and hedgerows and ditches.

so overcome   she did not hesitate   when the maintenance-
man   came to fix her heating   spoke through the door-
grill   but lifted the chain   she wrung her hands
crying   *the president has been shot*   stood in his white boiler-
suit   bag of heavy tools forgotten in hand   and stared
likewise at the screen   the motorcade broken
like a child's kicked line of cars   a shock shared
is more supportable   she was grateful not be alone
after the death arrived   he excused himself   work must be done
though new frontiers die   the debt collector must be paid
apartments must be made warm   for single girls in lonely Boston
JFK's city   through a halfopen door he watched   the motorcade
in playback   Jack smiling   and Jacqueline's proud face clear
of blemish nothing could stop   the next second's   horror
while with his other bloodstreaking eye   he watched disappear
his ordinary dull appearance from the bathroom's silver mirror
though he fought the spell   when the wolfbane blooms
under the high moon   even saints lock themselves apart
and chain their doors   something   loped through the room
as if it were snow   dry blood   tracks Jackie's skirt

Within your palm, ordinary and undowned,
I found no pentagram,
no star; your eyes stayed clear and cool
in the full moon; you did not disappear
in a silver mirror; I saw that your ears,
when you took off your fur hat,
and shook out your hair, were small
and rounded: all was normal: where
were the signs we would be bound

by the same rabid wound: lycanthropy?
When wolfbane blooms under a high full moon,
again, baying the moon, the pull
of a friendly, lighted house, with creches, fires,
catches you! For our benighted desires turn
inward, gnaw thighbones' human loss. No wonder,
under the strain, the cross-infection
courses round us like the cycle of rain, forever;
my cough in August is your fever in September;
sore, stye, migraine, pain in chest or back
attack us alternately. Always you or I
are visiting a sick-room. Nor could we live,
                              black and white witches,
but that we weave tight stitches for our wounds:
are pain and anodyne, pus and affection,
transplant, rejection, virus, antibody,
                              scald and lint.

'Even a man who says his prayers
before he sleeps each night,
may turn to a wolf when the wolfbane blooms
and the moon is high and bright.'

Chaos took one sharp bite at you,
invisibly he sped;
before your smile clamped to its mouth
the poison spread.

Soon as your blood rained on my skirt
like beast marks upon snow,
I knew you were in a forest where
to enter is to go

at once into its desolate heart;
none skirts its outer birches,
but penetrates past human call
to the black larches.

A change so absolute demands
more than these sinister
slight variations in your face,—
the cold—the stare—the leer.

Though I shall love you even till death,
if you returned tonight,
I'd bolt the door to your footfalls,
I'd shudder at your sight.

CONNEMARA

So many thousand eyes
—children's, perhaps, or lovers',
blue or grey as the clouds shuffle—
open in their sleep to me,
and close again,
their dream uninterrupted.

Or the one eye, always.

KILPECK

(On the outside of Kilpeck Church, Herefordshire, is a celtic gargoyle consisting of head and hands which are holding open a huge vagina; it is known locally as the Whore of Kilpeck.)

Four calendars rule Kilpeck
    village of church and sheep
between Wales and England past
and present four rhythms
like the church's four winds
The calendar of the sun
    its stormy rising spewing out lambs
    splayfooted by their ewes
The calendar of the saints
    spewing out Love from his tomb
    lamb of god uncertain on his feet
    his shroud like wool tufting the brambles
The calendar of the moon
    ripening the graves' and the castlewalls'
    poison-berries   bristling rare cottages' black
    black mountain cats
The calendar of the whore
    sowing the dead with ovarian seeds
    two weeks later dowsing them with blood

This stone cunt stretched wide by stone-hands
is as unfathomably black as the bird-pecked eyes of the sheep-
carcass on the hillside away from the sheltered flock
and twenty yards off her lamb
under the shadow of the crow
who pecks kills pecks
they sow the clean hills with furrows of flesh-stink

The calendars are dissonant
but once in a Great Year
they are in harmony
and then
under the full moon
  under the spouting seeds
    of the fullness of the whore's desire
      under the bells of resurrection
        the dead rise
        and couple with each other
        and with the priest and worshippers
        the sons of god come down and couple
        with the daughters of men hair tumbling from
        easter bonnets on the pews and overturned
        gravestones and the pasturing
        hillside a prayer of goodwill
        to all men and peace on earth rises
        from the threshing congregation's congress
        and the stone-cunt's red living lips
        turn upwards and sing
        a hymn of pure love
        in a pure soprano over the
        white mountains

NUDE WITH A RED HANDBAG

This menstruous nude with handbag red and stuffed
hurls it with all her sorrows at my head.
My menstruous nude with handbag stuffed and red
has with her air of walking naked bluffed

the world to think she bears her self alone.
Now, what cargo of deadweights, ballast, pours from her
flowering-open handbag falling through air,
sunspot engendering storms, collapsing sandstone!

She who's my trapped my trappist model makes
her own self-portrait, mixing blood with air,
she laughs and weeps to see her certain failure.
Loveletters tumbling from her palette-box

are slender tombstones, ancient fever-charts.
I turn to console her, turn to dry her tears . . .
Already in fallopian sky her satellite veers
to the dark, the start of the crescent. She squats,

absorbed in perilous delphic mysteries,
like one plugging a hole with dynamite;
then puts our love back on, no longer tight;
caresses, smiles, surprised at my surprise.

Once more she is my Lucy of the solstice,
madonna light, emerging from the pilot-
cabin in her guise of the blue stewardess
to hi-jack me from my false flight.

Almost she has forgotten that another
fruitless month has fallen from the calendar.
She gathers up her bag and it is slender.
Its clasps join smoothly as we move together.

It seems to her so clear that any nude
who lugs from death to death a stuffed red bag,
and turns each moon into a blistered hag,
must be allowed her cave of solitude.

HAIKU SEQUENCE

(Nape)
Subtle womanscent
God smelt and approved
even on creation's wrist.

Ghosts. Who taught you
to teach me to kiss
just-behind-the-ear?

Your tenderest inch
any beast's breath could stir
if you did not turn.

With time to spare. Your
pleased turned-away languor
pleases me. Slow thaw.

Your back tenses where
you can't guess where
I can't guess where to land.

Nationalised: rich
seams tapped here
do not make fortunes elsewhere.

Prevented, re-tracing spine,
lips find that blizzards
have buried tracks.

Delighted tongue ravishing
your ear wears like all
males a crude sheath.

(Armpit)
House of Bernarda Alba.
Absorbing, cloistral.
Vulva without doors.

Ear deep-tongued: if
my brain had a Bartholin's Gland
it would be flooded.

Clothed in earrings,
you disengage to strip yourself
submissively naked.

Lazarus-mouth pressed
to this world's black centre
takes his time rising.

Rising, surfacing
with a gasp, I must kiss—
share you with you.

You extract a wet
clinging hair from your mouth:
snake biting its own tail.

His engorgement,
this climbing stretchmark,
unbroken vertical.

Long nails cup and
threaten my manhood:
make me your priest.

I'd live gladly off
your five exudations,
those loaves and fishes.

Ten fingers join hands, dance
in the stifling-hot,
resting arena.

Teeth clamped to my nipple,
you stir
lust out of anger.

Lacquered nail, cold, indulgent,
pierces the anus:
a queen in Soho.

Thighs grip as they lose
the river they will
not wade in twice.

(Interrupt)
Light from receding
galaxies can't keep
pace with itself.

Tell her the stain
on your dress came
from gathering whitecurrants.

I'm abandoned! you whisper-smile,
eyes closed. Face plain,
hair matted, after love.

Only orifice too
intimate to touch or
kiss: nostrils.

Your middle-finger,
workshy aristocrat,
feels my tongue most.

You, in my pyjama-coat, dropping
spoons: yawning
slut, lust's anagram.

Flecked with red, a white-
packed ashtray invokes
your late guest.

(alba)
Alone
Lying
By your
Anxious flight.

Where the zip caught
your throat, two perfect
fangmarks. Sleep safe tonight.

We look in vain for
those comforting roadsigns
headlights conjure.

Like a motorway's
ill-signed sliproad
somewhere I lost you this time.

Your watching the youth
watching brisk towelled breasts
stiffen, stiffens me.

Eyes jealous even of
the ground's glimpse of flesh-
scything suspenders.

Unreal. In the train
I lift my finger to smell
your faint fingerprint.

Stretchmarks round your
breasts, on your mind,
slowly, slowly fade.

Siamesetwin, newly-stitched,
you jump in sleep.
Your lost self cries out.

On Yeats' tower. The
wind floated your skirt.
Goodbye, wild swan.

(Anniversary)
Joyous laughter. Absurd diners.
Control. Cointreau.
Cunt-roll. Canticle.

(Museum-skeleton with arrow-head)
Ribs and blade: one.
So will love's blade
outlive the flesh it pierced.

Our cigarette afterglows
in car window.
Star-shower from Capricorn.

Seventeen wild strokes.
So much passion needs
your containing scabbard.

RED-SHIFT

If the heavens were not recessive,
galaxies fading in a lemming-flight,
the night-sky, fit for angels only,
would be infinity's pure blinding light.

And you and I, breaking our kiss, we needed
the gulfs of black that spun from our drawn breath.
Brightly our love shone, because Love receded;
we saw the Plough of time; Orion, death.

GRETCHEN

Eternal woman
leading me on:
always your thighs cloven by
violence or tenderness
rape you.

Your eyes attract tears
as a moor-village, rain,
(blue-ringed always, the horizon);
or as the maddened windscreen wiper,
mesmerized snowflakes,
that break against the glass, are winnowed,
and break again.

Lightning-conductor of tragedy,
you absorb all suffering, all
forked energy,
and remain
untouched.

TRAWL

O fisher-girl,
when the shoal is brought in,
the rich white harvest
leaping and dying on the shore,
and beginning to give off
the smell of decay,
your shoulderblades
pale hungry fins
turn away,
your long, wading thighs
silently weep.

'TO LOUISA IN THE LANE'

When Hardy and Louisa in the Lane
(*the jump of the hare, says the Kama Sutra*)
passed, it mattered not that never again
(*the peacock's foot, says the Kama Sutra*)

Would he see her white muslin aching by.
(*the congress of the deer, says the Kama Sutra*)
A moment can dominate memory.
(*the line of jewels, says the Kama Sutra*)

'Good evening,' he stammered. Their only word.
(*the congress of the cat, says the Kama Sutra*)
It is doubtful if poor Louisa heard
(*the broken cloud, says the Kama Sutra*)

As she hurried on, with head downcast.
(*the tiger's nail, says the Kama Sutra*)
But when Thomas Hardy breathed his last
(*a leaf of the lotus, says the Kama Sutra*)

After fifty more years of passions and throes,
(*the rubbing of the boar, says the Kama Sutra*)
The wheelruts and the thorned hedgerows,
(*the coral and the jewel, says the Kama Sutra*)

And Louisa, long in a Stinsford grave,
(*the mounting of the horse, says the Kama Sutra*)
Was the last he remembered of human love
(*the line of points, says the Kama Sutra*).

ALDERSHOT WIVES

Adventurers conscripted by bright adverts,

they too keep their square; all round the perimeter of
Montgomery Road, Alexander Drive, Haig Avenue and Wellington Road,
the colours of their regiment hang bravely, red
and white and blue,
in ten thousand gardens.
Grey-uniformed, the houses stand, stolid, on parade
always ready for inspection; the gas-stoves
blanco'd, floors polished like fire-
extinguishers. They too are fighting a war, though

they have not yet identified the enemy. Much laughter
in the Naafi stores disguises uneasiness, a sixth-sense
of defeat. A fifth-column lurks, a traitor, the war of nerves,
of waiting; the
repetitive manoeuvres,
making life by numbers. The dusty road, Officers
and Other Ranks, floated by childish shouts, are a
Troy of slow private pyres, a Thermopylae
of neurosis, a Somme of costly small advances

and withdrawals. The longed-for foreign posting is an
Arnhem; hoping to take the enemy by surprise, they find
that they are floating down into desert or rice-fields,
but still encased,
pincered, in their own skin, and
habits, and habits of others, collected obsessively
over the years like cigarette-
coupons. They must land to a
withering crossfire of them-

selves. Even when summer signals shirtsleeve order, the swim-
suited wives are still under siege. Their task, clinging like
identity-discs, to prime the weapons who prime the
weapons, to take
them, shot and dirty, in

the afternoon, pull them through in the silently
diligent bedspaces of the night,
and send them out shining and highmorale-ed
for the morning-muster. Four tarnished letters in

Quo fas et gloria ducunt, are the k-rations of sex.
No rescue-column, flamboyant and bugled, will come spurring
kicking up the sandgrain houses of the Thames Valley,
to rescue them;
or if they do, they'll find
that the defiant phalanx of bayonet-aerials
jutting over the battlements, glinting,
are held up by uncanny silence,
a gallant strategem, a last beau geste.

FAMILY HISTORY

Black mother, black mother,
black hair by the fire, knitting to make us neat-and-tidy,
"What does dying mean? will you ever die?"
"Not for years and years and donkey's years! I won't leave you!"
Letting me melt night-terrors in your two-humped bed,
Black mother, black mother,
anxious, painting the scratch when I fall.

Grey mother, grey mother,
stretching up to kiss me at the end of a leave you
spent mending khaki-clothes to keep me neat-and-tidy.
Wondering if I take the girl to my stained bed,
"If you got her into trouble, I would die."
Grey mother, grey mother,
anxious lest I fall.

White widow, white widow, trapped needle
in the black grooves of a dead turntable, you die
silenceshocked into us. Visited, if the children fall,
shrieking for us. Crocheting, the shrine kept neat-and-tidy;
lump in my throat as our full car leaves you
White widow, white widow
to photos round your wide one-humped bed.

Black widow, black widow,
plopped into the middle of our pain-sweet bed;
layer-out of yourself, your spindly limbs kept neat-and-tidy;
spinning your web of obscene wants. We can't leave you.
You clutch at our arms, shrieking lest you fall.
Black widow, black widow, black widow,
what does living mean? why don't you die?

LAKESIDE

'*Prove that you love me!*' she said, as a girl will.
'*Anything!*' the boy stammered. '*Anything? Then let me see
you walk the waves.*' He fished for inspiration in her eyes.
And walked. She gave him the spice of her lips, half-mockingly.

'*Prove that you love me! Change this water into wine.*'
She pointed to her pitcher, cracked in the heat of noon.
He lifted an arm. She drank, and hugged her ankles.
Gave him the wine of her tongue, and bit his own.

'*Prove that you love me!*' '*Anything.*' '*I'm hungry now.
Change this dry crust to a feast, and don't be long.*'
There were baskets to spare. She bared her small teeth in pleasure.
Spared him the roes her breasts—then away she sprang.

Hid herself in a rock. Tortured, he seized her.
But she wriggled like a lizard away. '*Prove
that you love me!*' A cripple was passing. '*Heal me him.*'
The cripple walked. For an instant his finger clove

the hill of frankincense, but again she twisted
out of his grasp, her laugh invaded by a gasp of pain.
She stood on the rock, goading, belly thrust forward.
'*Prove that you love me! Die for me,*' she said.

'*Die, and you can have this. Not unless.*' She kilted
her robe, pulled open the sepulchre to show the red
sand-flesh waiting. Speech and colour left his lips.
'*So you don't love me!*' She laughed, spat grossly, and fled.

Wandering to the shore, he helped the fishermen
with their nets; but his mind and his blood ran
on the frightening fount of energy that had leapt in him.
She bitched about homelong, blood splashing like menstrual wine

that flowered lemon-trees in her aimless wake;
forgot by dusk the strange shy clumsy boy,
knowing too well the power in her little finger
to stir such deeds, and more, when the devil was in her.

APOCRYPHA

From the shore the child
saw the telltale shimmer when
the casting boats were
blinded. 'Cast your nets on the
right,' he shouted. They did so.

Twelve years. Night was arched
by a dazzling white rainbow.
Joy and fear floated
him off, he was alpha and
omega; beginning, end.

The village empty,
he yielded to impulse.
Bent to the well, saw
the strange otherMary look
up, tense in silk, bewildered.

He tingled at a
touch of lips so light it was
less than the black streak
of a kingfisher, rising,
wrigglingsilver in its beak.

At Magdala. He
touched by chance the hem of her
skirt. Seven devils
rushed into him. Thirty coins
burnt a hole in his pocket.

She removed his hand,
and gazed over Galilee.
To make love to God!
She caught to her lips his five
wise fingers heavy with oil.

Thinking of her smile
of welcome, he walked over
the lake to meet her;
the hills took up their bed and
walked; the skeins dropped from the world.

She moved at her task
like breezes over the late
lake. Love tightened his
throat. Her good simple meal could
have fed five thousand of him.

An alabaster
box of fragrant ointment, tool
of her profession,
burst upon his tongue that churned
seeking the close-cauled stable.

Before the dawn broke,
they stirred in their sleep. Masts of
grey lolling boats were
three crosses. Each looked at the
loved face and did not know it.

Her cunt still pulsed. He
was already penitent.
'I come, to give you
life more abundantly.' Her
mockery cleansed him, teeth flashed.

Like a woman who
scours her house and makes endless
finds more delightful
than the trinket lost, his eyes
explored her for love's reason.

At Cana. Tense with
worry. Recriminations
flew. Then rain from the
south fell; as she stood up: through
her dress, a joyous winestain.

Always her garden
always easter, raised him, made
him stand humble, born.
He touched her back and she turned,
astonished, fingers testing.

He could not believe
he had risen again. He
lay in the arms of
Mary. Light as the blind he
touched all her redeeming holes.

In an agony
of masochism, he forced
her to relate all
the details of the strangers
who had eaten of her flesh.

Where she buried her
most passionate kisses the
stigmata of flowers
grew up, purple, long after
he had thought of them as dead.

Each month lilies bloomed
from the grave of her desires.
A half, waxing moon
on the cold lake. Her desires
were buds one coarse word could kill.

Full yellow moon shone
that the oars dripped silver.
There was no holding her back
she pressed him into her, moaned:
'take no thought for the morrow.'

Storms sawed her into
jagged waves of latesummer.
A half, waning moon.
She grew turgid, baleful. He
knew better than to still it.

It would still itself.
The moon disappeared, all but
an earthlight of him.
Half in relief, half despair,
the lakeside trees loosed red falls.

At the last moment
she tried to cut the nets she
had helped to cast, jack-
knifed her spasming loins. But
the son of God slipped from her.

He was a fisher
of men. Fishergirl, her pale
back turned from the drag-
nets swollen on the curved shore.
Her thigh wept a galaxy.

Tenderly he wiped
the glans free of its bud of
liquid. 'In there, one
the latchet of whose shoes I
am not worthy to unloose.'

At their heights he could
enter her again at once,
hard, this time sustain
it forever, repeating
the ninety-nine names of God.

Two Marys bent to
sponge his crucified breathing
flesh: breast, face, thighs, feet,
the circumcised organ of
excretion and genesis.

He stood in the red
sand which the sun's hourglass had
poured out. A snakeskin
hissed: *Thirty years. Halfway*. Poised
between sloughed skin and round stone.

At Bethany. One
netted him with her hair, one
watched. His breast sighed. What
tension was left to frot his
ever tumescent spirit?

He came to a fig-
tree that was barren, having
leaves but no fruit. He
called up an old image and
masturbated in its shade.

'Child from Nazereth,
you will not suffer me to
come to you. A mill-
stone of gravity hangs on
me.' Round, dust-ringed eyes stared up.

Meshes of her lids
iridescent in the dark.
She said to John, 'Cleave
a log and I find him still,
turn a stone and he is there.'

'No, no payment. You
saved my life.' She touched her bruised
cheekbone, raw scars. 'Why
did you visit me?' He drew
on the floor, smiled bitterly.

Her eyes shone at him
out of an oasis. He
said, 'You are the light
of the world. No man comes to
the mother except by you.'

He would cram thirty
years into three, climb a dark
splintered stairs, and by
the intensity of his
lust, lie with eternity.

VERONICA'S NAPKIN

Jesus, when he bore the cross,
Up the Dolorous Way stumbled and lurched;
A young girl, at her window, touched
To the quick of her heart at his distress,

Snatched up a napkin, and leaning out
And down, till the eastering slopes of her breasts
Stretched her child's-robe to bursting, pressed
The cloth to his forehead, rivered with sweat.

Startled, he stopped. For a moment she saw,
In close-up, the felon's bloodstreaked eyes,
Cruel tender mouth, parted in surprise.
He glimpsed a thin dark face withdraw

Within the inscrutible shutters. Though
She was pure as the lilies of the fields,
For a week, strange tremors and pricklings had swelled
As if some passion-flower would grow

But could not, her skin too marble-pure.
Now, noise shut out, in the cool chamber,
She pressed the towel to her maidenhair,
And wondered what fever it should cure,

Amazed with herself, ashamed. In bed
That night, her thighs kept it loosely held;
And dawn's bright bars on the floor revealed
To her joy, his features in brilliant red.

Three mornings the firstfruits of her womb
Gave Veronica's napkin his face in blood.
He carried her image in his head,
Clenched, through the turmoil of the tomb.

EDEN
(found-poem from the lips of Sean Thomas, aged 4)

When I kiss Eve
all the clothes dance
and all the boys jump up on to the roof
                              And
do you know what the dinner does?
The dinner comes down from the big school
then it lays itself on the tables
and eats itself up
Do you know what the plates do?
They gather themselves up
they go to Mrs Herd
they get into the washing-basin
they wash themselves
and they put themselves back on the shelves
                              And
do you know what the pictures do?
They come down
throw the old ones in the fire
then the crayons get out
pull out a piece of paper
they draw another picture
then the sellotape comes out of the cupboard
and sticks the pictures up
                              And
do you know what the school does?
The school pulls itself down
and builds itself up into a church

When I kiss Eve
magic-stuff comes
out through our mouths and

Do you know what the plants do?
They all die
then the seeds in the bag
come into the garden
then they pop into the ground

                                        And
do you know what the trees do?
They spring themselves down and die
the seeds walk about
in the mud
and the wind comes along and blows over them
and grows up into appletrees and
cherrytrees grow up
then some sunflowers came
and tulips came
and roses came
                              And and
do you know what the lights do?
They come down
the bulbs go to the shop
to buy another bulb
Do you know what the piano does?
The piano plays itself and
all the toys jump
and play with themselves
                              And
do you know what the sky does?
All the sky jumps down
in the night it did
the sun fell the wind dropped
and half the world fell down and
all the flies were dead
and all the wasps were dead
no more flies and no more wasps
                              And
                              And
                              And
do you know what the plates do?
They gather themselves up . . .

MUSIC STUDENT FIRST VIOLINIST
(in the Dvorak D Minor Symphony)

Anton, all the black notes of your symphony
Have swarmed into this girl's allegro hair.
Only the sluggard breves and minims stay
Trapped by the bars of the conductor's score.

Pours frozen from her crown's simple motif
A black cascade of glistening counterpoint
To where my gladly martyred eyes receive
Ten thousand quavers' barbed and startling points,
Where the taut canvas chairback lets it go.

So near, I could imprison with my hand
The tempting weight of that polyphony,
Tug her bent head back from the weaving bow.
There is a melody in each separate strand,
Had I a chance to study its great score;
Your temporal genius rendered spatially.

It is too short, this timeless hour. The time
To plumb its currents, ponder how it weaves
From the home minor to a major key
And brings it back, find if it joys or grieves
In its own ponderings of its own shut score,
Cannot be measured by the metronome,
Or clock, or pulse, or carbon in the rocks.

I catch its shampoo's faintly lurking theme
And sense the recent crisis—she attacked
Lacklustre strands with demons in her hands.
All was dismay—will it be right in time?
She hacked its knots before the fire. Tonight
The whole performance is in place, exact;
Blue-hazed with static electricity.
Her soul's in music, music in her hair.

Symphony of her darkest attribute.
She'll wrap it in a scarf, and disappear.
A tube will hold her and her buried stream.

Since art is less than life, agree
That I do right, amidst the coughs, to hear
No music but its waist-long cataract.
She will express you just as passionately
When all the white notes of your symphony,
Unlike the black notes dead within the score,
In the rich coda of the major key
Have swarmed into this girl's adagio hair.

WOMAN AND HARP

. . . Gypsy glissandi shiver as her nail
Modulates the vertebrae of gold.
Touch light as this could make an angel fall.
And now she fans the ember to a fire,

As plucks the wind, night-secrets without words,
Inflamada, soledad. From the fold
Of her black dress, what a black flash of birds.
Swallows! Golondrinas! Corazons of desire!

And our dry spirits, caught in its inferno,
Which no one touch has lit, but manifold
Circling caresses, have the silent glow
Of a dark forest burning everywhere.

Grasses of silence, tree-heights of applause.
The harp is fire, the intrepid fingers cold;
In her art's land she only heeds its laws;
And with an air more magic than the air

She's played, her hands compose an attitude
Cutting the echo dead . . . This sense of songs
Perfected only when they end; the joy

With which all time's canzones have pursued
A burnt-out rhapsody; she, silencing
The flame raised by her palms, entrances me,

As though a dazzling nude
Races the heart more when her brown arms fling
Over the flickering torse a canopy;

The love she makes is to her solitude;
Her hands upon the resonating strings,
She leans into its eloquent reply.

A LEGEND

At St Anthony's
Head, they pointed to the sign
    of the fish. The first

century panel in
an ancient temple; the ship,
    phoenician. Ogham

characters told how
he had been wrecked here, a ship's
    carpenter. The bell

is phoenician too,
in the forgotten, hardest
    cast, wroth bronze. It fell

and was not broken,
miraculously; its note
    still virgin. I left

the tudor hotel
with a girl as sweet scented
    as saffron. Round the

first turning in the
narrow road towards Truro,
    I saw him. He was

as though awaiting
the car, and flashed a dazzling
    smile of love. I stopped,

and he sat where the
girl sat; she merged into the
    april hedge. Spring was

late, unseasonal
cold blew from the east; hawthorn
    not broken. He looked

young enouth to be
my son, ruddy in hair, face
    deep-freckled. 'Drive, drive—'

he said. 'I wanted
to see it all again just
once. And you.' So I

drove, recklessly, tears
streaming, through the landscape he
had walked through. He pressed

the images like
transfers, hungrily, to his
unstressed brow. Minestacks

and engine-houses
swept by, whitewashed terraces,
wind-plastered. 'Do you

remember how on
this hill, but a mile from home,
John Arthur Bray took

out the first of his
twenty pasties, said he smelt
the sea-air? He laughed

his laugh that is like
wroth bronze, rough tones struck from a
fine, clear soul. And the

granite day streamed sun
suddenly, waves of it surged
across gorse. 'I know,'

I said, 'so little
of you, your earlier years;
I yearn to.' His eyes

grew tender. 'Assume,'
he said, 'I skimmed the sea with
stones, kissed girls. Love this

land you shipwrecked in.
Through it I shall stay with you.
Keep faith with it; grow

down into it like
the cheesewring, though the ground is
quarried at your feet.'

TWO AT CASTLE DOR
sixteen variations on a legend

Yes they are out of tune
they walk without speaking
neither will break silence
but ask them if they should
part even for an hour
and they will not listen
there is even a kind
of perplexing joy in
this walking together
at their furthest apart
of knowing that time must
inevitably bring
them more closely apart
till her red lips greet him
somewhere in green meadows
these lovers in their blue

Always there are other
lovers in the time-mists
whose love was absolute
without shadow he thought
they too walked here seeking
the man whose hair did not
comb out the maid who did
not sweat the nine maidens
dancing on a sunday
in a circle to ward off
cold and rain two broken
hearted three lonely three
plain one beautiful but
waiting her period
gazed at the mystic stone
druids in a sun-ring

Shut in the one closet
together for the first
time in a year clothes are
at first congealed in frost
dumbstruck and estranged silk
by cloth unused to the
luxury to unpack
to produce a small week-
long household are frightened
by so many days nights
silver shoes within their
prince's feel trapped and his
appalled by ownership
gradually the melt
begins coat and cloak touch
robes find they are dancing

Silted and turgid he
dredges from her past love-
objects she despises
she smiles and is silent
outwitting her gaoler
again the river runs
she knows his three shadows
who lurk in the orchard
whenever she steps out
to meet the dream she stroked
in the forgotten dawn
knows who will leap at them
at the slightest error
violence a rare spy
sullenness a likelier
passion an unfailing

For both a splinter throbs
forever in the brain
they can forget their own
but suffer when they see
the other sigh with grief
it is that they exist
always on the pure
oxygen of a tent
and the invisible
helmet enclosing them
they long for atmosphere
for humble gravities
they might be on the moon
or drifters in dead space
hooked to the encapsuled
potion their loins are rocks

Before they are well out-
doors the day is turning
the cloudless blue through the
bedroom window is now
threatened from the west with
black the first spots of rain
grope her face like the blind
what is love she thinks but
a succession of days
ending before they start
his throat is razor-cut
spots his collar with blood
she has lost illusions
her love is balancing
tilting like the day is
oiled as a logan stone

She does not satisfy
him love her for an hour
she will stay virginal
his thoughts will be away
in apple-avalon
his private paradise
the hands that are playing
his back with cool fingers
like a stringed instrument
are not the hands he wants
tonight he does not know
what hands he needs tonight
hands dirtier coarser
but bearing the same name
her eyes wide she senses
surreptitious onan

She cried look up look up
there right above our heads
I thought it was a lark
but the sky was filled with
the birds that nested in
their eyes and flew up when
the sky was that cold blue
and when he was stretched back
sighting along her arm
he would have found the source
of that pure melody
if there were a gold thread
somewhere where her left hand
leaned on his shoulder some-
where by her nape-hair the
axis of balancing

At the cheesewring quarry
she picks up from the ground
a stone and gives it him
see how perfect it is
immaculate shining
the separate elements
black and white have grown in-
extricably welded
some gigantic storm has
hurled the hurlers down where
they lie in pure circles
in the mist they cannot
tell if the cheesewring slabs
vaster as they mount are
incredibly stable
cubes or rocking hugely

Looking at the boulders
balancing each other
the sunset skyline sheathed
in rock like two blazing
swords one squat one slender
meeting in a dark point
more a blindspot in light
than dark point knowing that
these huge granite masses
the touch of a finger
sets swaying she resolves
to put her reticence
and her indifference
between them like a sword
that they may sway ever
two and yet one logan

She is starkly awake
contemplating his sleep
is oppressed by ageing
by laughterlines paunches
grey hairs he is half-way
that thought sinks into her
from now every moment
indistinguishable
else flies black and not white
and flies faster faster
what is to become of
them and what is to come
time after time trying
vainly to screw themselves
tight to each other's flesh
in a thread that leaves them

He must read alone for
her hair to be doing
she comes shining lacquered
glossy coils of music
for the day to revolve
crackles with electric
as he takes it in hands
gently and tenderly
gently she removes them
but is all smiles he
blesses her resilience
she is all counterpoint
no strand is obvious
he is a diamond as
the wind starts to play her
stone stylus and maiden

Each time she devours him
totally to eclipse
she must let her light fade
for him to shine again
no he cannot love her
glum as an old priest in
her lap dwarf with the same
name is a dead man it
will take long to revive
with her warm embraces
he is fighting her off
with granite chilliness
the ship with brave white sails
approaching its harbour
turns a keel flying back
cutting the drowned valley

Her eyes in her pale face
he thought have the stillness
the turquoise of the lakes
under the clay-cones' grey
abandoned silica
as restful as secret
from the passing strangers
who hunt the frenetic
his dark eyes and his voice
go down into me through and
through rob me yet give me
me myself restore me
myself and rob me she
saw along that rivercombed
coast steel-clawed dredgers plunge
into estuary sounds

Sources below sources
can one ever find the
holy spring where a love
or a legend began
in a strand of hair light
enough for a swallow
to carry across seas
they walk under a tor
feet sinking in bright green
hands locked to help founder
each other and search for
the source among many
where the inaudible
treacherous lushness
becomes the unsilenced
tone-poem of river

Two cannot look up at
stars for long together
he thinks of the boy who
a child of these moors
lay back upon his hands
neglecting his duties
the sheep in the dark pale
as the crab nebula
he was to discover
a planet from a sense
of the stars' emptiness
their yearning for something
to complete their blessing
night turned over his tors
pleiades flying like
birds deeper and clearer

These lovers in their blue
robes find they are dancing
druids in a sun-ring
passion an unfailing
potion their loins are rocks
oiled as a logan stone
surreptitious on an
axis of balancing
cubes or rocking hugely
in a thread that leaves them
two and yet one logan
stone stylus and maiden
cutting the drowned valley
into estuary sounds
tone-poem of river-
birds deeper and clearer

LOGAN STONE

if it were one
stone it would not be magical
if it were two stones the attrition of
rain cutting into its natural weakness too well
it would not be magical if its massif could be set
trembling neither two nor one for a moment only say
the logging-point of night-fall it would be magical yet
not miraculous small worlds may be born of such magic
but that it can go on and on without ceasing dazzling
the spectator with immobile motion neither two nor one
neither one nor two doomed and unshakable on its point
of infinity that is the miracle   to be so weak
a finger logs it what constant strength
what force it takes to be a
logan-
stone you and I what cold applied
granite-fire logging on weakness no storm can move us

PENWITH

Did flint tools or alone the driving rain
complete its holy paradox: granitic
yet sensitive as the joint of a bone?

Nine maidens petrified for sabbath dancing
or sun-discs crouched in an altar-less ring,
in a misty field the sea's whetstone hones
to a sharp blade; the sun tests it, aslant.

On the humped moor's spine, consumptive miners
turned aside from their plod home to crouch and pass
through the men-an-tol, the ring of granite.

I am the loganstone a cloud can alter,
inert mass trembling on a compass-point;
I am the men-an-tol, the wind's vagina;
I am the circle of stones grouped around grass.

BOTALLACK

Needles flake off into the blue air. Listen.
In the August silence, on the bare cliff-path, you can fling
a stone and it will not break the silence, but you can hear
the wedges and drills of erosion hammering
in a silence that is uproar, beneath the wrecking Brissons.

The sea might ring to a finger today. Bone-china.
Without the drama of weathers, no flowers or trees
to mask time with recurrence, time's raw nerve
shows through here like an outcrop of tin. A peace
that is the acceptance of defeat reigns. Miners

trekked this vertical, nerves tempered granite;
at their head, candles —defeat —disaster— dowsed,
to stride out under the sea as courageous,
poor in all but tall tales the ocean housed,
as their methodist Christ walked out upon it.

Botallack locks against too strong a force;
blue-framed, nettled engine-house, cliff-set. The logan stone
of me is here. Bal-maidens spalling ore
for bread feared not the plunge. Why should I alone
stride ahead of the flood, on a white sea-horse?

Down in those spirit-heights, if the guttering
candles failed, kind-
ly light amidst the encircling gloom, one man
guided them unfailingly through blackwaters. He was blind.
In the country of the blind, that man was king.

OLD WOMAN

Alert only to
draughts, dangerously balanced coals,
—poking out her stick to prod them back—
quivering and squealing at sparks
that will burn her alive
if she can be called alive,
buried in her functions,
waiting for the next time she must
hobble to urinate,
for he next time she must
insert eye-drops, take tablets,
roll down her stockings immodestly, in a parody
of striptease, to embrocate her joints,
or gum-nibble tea-sopped food.
The real world is snowed under;
these are the base-camps that
mark out the day's wilderness
that she crosses
motionlessly, bent on her two sticks like a polar walker,
trembling each second for the crack of disaster;
each waste imperceptibly bleaker.

But at bed-time, her blinding eyes seem to brighten.
She gathers up, stocks up
her bags and baskets
full of the night's provisions,
thermos-flasks and biscuits and medicaments,
and I carry them up for her
as her parents did
at picnic-times and tea-treats,
while she runs ahead of me, pigtails flying,
races shrieking with delight, reckless
of scratches and sudden shafts,
or to meet her sweetheart
who will conceive me under the shy stars.

MEDITATION ON LINES FROM THE METHODIST HYMNAL

glad tidings
of great joy
I bring

I remember how my father's galed
unparalleled
laugh, a split-off boulder, spilled
landslips of gaiety round us till all voices tumbled
a mountain through the cinema. All knew him there. The child
squirmed, embarrassed. Later, his laughter, song, failed.
Wrily he let himself be borne through the mild
operation, towards death,
as through rugby-turnstiles.

pleasant are
thy courts
above

With three flowers and tears to spare, I hunt-
for the grave of my three spinster aunts.
If only the churchyard were luminescent,
neon flashing from all the graves that want
a tear from me. I find it, pinch a jampot
from a grave with two jampots. Hack at
its jungle. My son dances on the cleared plot,
blind to the subliminal advert.
l stop him, think better, persuade him to start
dancing again. Three flowers, and a grammersow, in a jampot.

there is a
green hill
far away

Two brown carns, crowned with the thorns of gorse.
To the coombe between, John Wesley bore his cross,
and the tinners let him nail them to the promise
of more than their underground ships' harvest of loss
—two coins for their black lade of ores:
catastrophe in granite gales, or the castaway ebb of phthisis.
Built him the village's only great house,
bleak-stoned, unceremonious.

love divine
all loves
excelling

An aunt I had who all her life would run
from one task to another, (in a photo I've seen one
young man with her, and laughed), hobbling through the chicken-run
of her peck-pecking invalid sisters, working nun
among contemplatives, yanking up lisle stocking over dirt-brown
spindly shanks as she ran;
broke the web spiders spun
in blackberry hedges. Sin
touched her up once in a vestry, her organist father. Otherwise
                                    none.
'Are your meals alright?' whispered, her lonely race of lovedivine
                              well-run.

sow in the
morn thy seed

In postman's knock I did not understand,
standing in the sundayschoolroom's damp porch, the wind
off the north cliffs rattling the outside door, the hand
of an impish pander
(the elders drank tea) patient on the latch, that the bland
as cream daughter of St John wanted to feel my hand
break the seal of her unopened.
I knowing only the geography of the Holy Land
burned.

deep in
unfathomable
mines

Let go at last,
unsafety-lamped, I courted disaster
deliriously in the dark's build-up of inflammable gas.
Skipped down shafts of sublimated lust.
Returning home pilot-light burning in the black waste
of midnight the riggings of a score of wrecks were cast
up in the starlight of the landrocks, their hulls fast
in the landlocked sea, the past.
In one, the whole Cornish male voice choir was lost:
Wheal Harmony. I paused listening; then again crossed
the left-half-done hysterectomy of addits. At the last
turning, a horse farted strangely, hindquarters bulked
            dreaming, above me. I pressed
on: a flask, sandwiches of meat or paste,

when I
survey the
wondrous cross

waiting up anxiously. Care swung, lanterns in a storm,
wrecking me in saving me from harm.
Summer-time, A30 tourist time,
I half-return, take up my childhood name,
'Donald'. Who's that disyllabic nice boy? I'm
the bright boy who went upcountry. I'm
without a village wall. Sipping vodka and lime

did e'er such
love and
sorrow meet

I stand in the pub, selfconscious;
the choir of beerdrinkers, harmonious,
slant towards each others' mouths, eyes, as scant thorntrees
of the north cliffs slant to the gentler sloping trees
of the south coast. Draw strength and give it. The voice
of my father struggles up gloomy levels of me to match
            their joyfulness.
They would be lost without the cross.
I dress my poems in a dry-room of loss.

feed me till I want no more Phthisis in men's lungs, arthritis in women's bones, scrape
sockets of dry desire. Old widows, tea-addicted, without hope
this side the grave. Preparing their crones of sleep,
undoing, unlacing, undenturing. Old mineshafts the present
            can't escape.
Old women secretly undermined from birth by landscape.
Old mineshafts secretly racked like the old women who rape
me. Limbs grow out of shape
as housewalls subside. I can't escape
contagions in my native air. My landscape
is this shrunk coombe's postmenopausal cuntscape.
At my betraying absence I weep,

the day thou gavest lord is ended father, and with pious hapless hands pluck
a year's weeds from your grave. You were struck
down by the dank
calvery air you loved. I thought just a gland was sick.
Each night you wreck
your stone, come rain or snow seek
me far north of the Tamar. You choke
on blood and breath, exit before I wake.
In my mirror, the tender teethmark.
Your loving empty hands take
me, wreckers' treasure. Someone must thrust a stake
into my heart before your willpower breaks.

the seed-time and the harvest 'But naturally!' laughs the out-of-work analyst.
'You are seeking the boy you never were.' Sails rest,
temporary as butterflies, on the estuary. I have confessed
I usually fall for women with small breasts.
Shouting it out; for he is deaf as a post.

and pour contempt on all my pride Out of the blue of the scudding land's end sky,
in my second, dodging, darkglassed holiday,
five miners slouch down the seaward way,
croust-bags swinging, towards old Geevor mine. 'They
must be pot-holers.' Reddled with their trade, eyes and
            teeth cheerily
gleam. We pull in to see.
They stare at the tourists staring at them. I look away.
The guidebook says: 'they heard the seabed stones rattle
            above their gallery.'
Converted to a meadery,
a gaunt Wesleyan chapel. We sit
by scented fingerbowls and candlelight
in bottles, crouched over barreltops, and eat
scampi and chips, drink the honeymoon drink. A glint

of family madness in her eyes, my love talks about
dying. 'Fuck death!' I spit,
and slide my hand along the pew, under her skirt.
Invasive as a celtic saint,
my finger opens her like the spine of a new testament.

**and glory
shone around**
The granite shoulder of the penwith moor wears heather
purple as the cloak of Joseph of Arimethea
when he rode on muleback up from the island harbour,
the 'hoar rock in the woods'; the young ship's carpenter
riding beside him. They came to stare
at the blackrobed barbarians streaming the precious ore.
A grey fist with a raised index finger,
the ruined engine-house of Ding-Dong mine still stands there
today high on the jagged height of the pagan moor.
We have bruised the heather to stare
at men-an-tol, holed stone in the ground: curer
of scrofula, barrenness, broken heart, or wart.
Though it says naked, in the guidebook, stuff that.
Clothed as I am, I'll squat
and squirm through it.

**where shall
my wandering
soul begin**
Seined by a million bones,
my soul begins
here in the stamping-house of bronze.

**rock of ages
cleft for me**
At Botallack. The engine-house of the knackt bal
overleans the cliff-edge. More beautiful,
even, than before man's depradation brought toil
and scars to this loneliest wild heel
of Cornwall. Blue day, winds from the murderous Brissons flail
her light dress, my shirt. The sea folds and unfurls
endlessly its spray. Ancestral
miners trail
before and behind us down the gullhewn perilous
path, vanish underground undersea. Bal-
maidens surround us, spall
the ore with long hammers. They loved their hammered hailed
rock. Their love was need. It failed.
(Cornish: Love) Lies like kerensa beyond recall,
like the makers of the cromlechs on the hill.
From failure is this beauty born. My girl
blends with the chough-calls her light southern drawl.

Our passing call
has changed Botallack, brings a new love, however frail,
to overlay kerensa. The tidal pull
brings new lives in like wrecks, as hedges fall
away to sea. The celts were strangers. Our fingers spall,
in unison, ore beyond bronze. No alloy is final.